BARNHART MEMORIAL LIBRARY
BURRILL BLVD., DIX, N.Y.

CORNELL
GRAMETIC VINYL LIBRARY
X, N. Y.

ONE LORD—ONE FAITH

ONE LORD ONE FAITH

AN EXPLANATION

BY

VERNON JOHNSON

LONGMANS, GREEN AND CO.
55 FIFTH AVENUE, NEW YORK
1929

COPYRIGHT, 1929
BY VERNON JOHNSON

FIRST EDITION

MADE IN THE UNITED STATES OF AMERICA

"Jesus! I would so love him,
Love him as He has never yet been
loved." *St. Thérèse.*

VERITAS DOMINI MANET IN AETERNUM
(Ps. 117; 2)

PREFACE

I AM publishing this book as a little explanation, in answer to the many letters which I have received asking for the reason for my action in becoming a Catholic. After months of weary struggling, when at last I saw the coming end to be inevitable, I began to put some notes together. I did this in order to clear my own mind and to have something written to fall back upon in those moments, which I knew must come, when my human feelings might overwhelm my reason. But I did so also in order to have some explanation ready for others, should it be necessary.

From the countless letters which I have received, it is clear that some such explanation is required; and so, very humbly and with great diffidence, I offer this to those dear friends who have loved and trusted me so wonderfully and who are so completely at a loss to understand why I have acted as I have.

Thus it is in no sense a polemic, covering all possible argument for and against, but just a very simple account of those particular events and reasons which led me to take this step.

It will be seen that the supreme reason, behind all

7

others, was that I could not resist the claim of the Catholic Church to be the one True Church founded by Our Lord Jesus Christ to guard and teach the truth to all men till the end of time. She alone claims to be infallibly guided by the Holy Spirit in her teaching: she alone possesses the authority and unity necessary for such a Divine Vocation; and she alone, in the Papacy, gives any effective and working meaning to the position of St. Peter in Scripture. It was the positive fact of the Catholic Church from which I could not escape.

Thus the state of the Church of England was a very secondary difficulty and only served to confirm my growing belief in the Catholic Church. The Prayer Book controversy was, to me, more a symptom than anything else; though serious, it was never so serious, to me, as modernism. Modernism, I saw, as I came to understand it better, was clearly destroying the true conception of, and belief in, the Personality of Christ and His Godhead—the Foundation Truth of the Christian Religion.

It is inevitable that I should be charged with desertion. I can only remind people that I was always in the thick of it. Difficulties did not affect me seriously until I came to question the whole position, not because of the difficulties but because I had seen something else which I was increasingly conscious was Divine.

I first met with the Catholic Church as a living reality at Lisieux in 1925. Readers may wonder why it was that it was so long before I took the final step.

The answer is that I am just a very ordinary Englishman; and, as such, I had within me, bred in my very bones, all the dread and fear and suspicion of Rome, and the distrust of what I considered ecclesiastical intrigue and Italian government—the latent hostility which I had inherited as part of the usual English education and tradition—all this I had to a quite extraordinary degree.

Thoroughly insular, I had never been abroad till 1925. And, so far as I can remember, till then I had only spoken twice to a Catholic priest, and then both times only casually. I had never been to a Catholic service, and had only occasionally looked in at Catholic churches. I say all this because people generally, and Catholics specially, do not seem to realize how utterly separated from one another Catholicism and Anglo-Catholicism are. So far as I was concerned, till 1925, they were entirely separate worlds.

I had never troubled about the Catholic Church and was completely satisfied with Anglo-Catholicism. It was not till I began to realize that "Rome might possibly be right" that I began to realize also how deep-set in my own subconscious self was this distrust of "Rome."

Thus, even after things became intellectually fairly clear, it was all something outside me. I was still bound in the bonds of prejudice and fear.

From the other side, another reason which held me back was the overwhelming shrinking from taking a course which must give such pain to countless souls whom I loved so dearly. Also I was convinced that I ought not to lay down a ministry which had been so greatly blessed so long as there was any possibility of being able to go on.

As to where the turning point comes in any great decision it is always desperately difficult to determine.

It seems to me that, when that moment approaches one is so overwrought and weary with the struggle that one only realizes that a certain step is inevitable, and one just gets up and staggers towards it in the dark.

To those who have always been Catholics the argument of this book will seem absurdly simple, and much of it may seem overdrawn. They will, I know, realize that this is written in a transitory stage, and expresses my mind at this particular moment, when still only on the threshold. To them the gain so far outweighs the loss. But they are within, they know the Church and it is their home. To the soul outside, groping towards the light, it is just leaving home and countless dearly loved scenes and faces and deliberately stepping into exile: it is an act of naked faith: it is only later on that that soul can possibly realize that the apparent place of exile is its home.

If, in the later pages of this book, I have seemed to

lift the veil too much—it is done with the greatest diffidence and for two reasons:

First, to let those countless souls who have shewn me their love and trust realize that, throughout it all, it was just the consciousness of the infinite pain and distress that my action must cause them that was such an overwhelming sorrow.

Secondly, because it has been my experience of those souls who have taken a similar step that it is not an easy action, taken in a moment of emotion, but a path of very great suffering, taken almost entirely in the dark, only illumined by the certainty which comes by faith.

Vernon Johnson

September 8th, 1929
at 9a Albert Road, N.W.1.

CONTENTS

PART I

LISIEUX

PART II

PART III

PART I

PART I

CHAP. I: *THE BEGINNINGS*

IT was in the late autumn of 1924. I was standing in an Anglican convent and holding in my hands a book, the autobiography of St. Thérèse of Lisieux. It had been put into my hands by the Reverend Mother of the Convent to which I had been sent to take a Retreat.

I had protested, saying that that sort of book did not interest me, that I had looked into it some years before in a (Roman) Catholic shop and had come to the conclusion that it was sentimental and artificial, un-English, and that it was just another Roman Catholic scheme for exciting devotion amongst the public, and that I distrusted it. The Reverend Mother replied that I ought not to say that. So I submitted and took the book.

At that time I had been ordained and ministering in the English Church as an Anglo-Catholic for over thirteen years. I had been for ten years in an Anglican brotherhood. And yet the (Roman) Catholic Church had never presented itself as a problem to my mind. So far as I had thought of her I had regarded her as the greatest indeed of all the

Christian bodies but one which had made many and great mistakes—notably her insistence on the Papal claims. These mistakes completely separated her from the Church of England, and vaguely, I suppose, I hoped that she would one day find her proper place in the final reunion of Christendom which, however, was too far off to worry about very seriously.

Many who read this will be amazed that one could go on ministering for so many years as an Anglo-Catholic and yet never come in closer contact with the Catholic Church. But it really is a very ordinary experience. The reason is this: in the lives of most English people to-day the Catholic Church is no more than a name. In so far as she touches their lives she only does so indirectly.

To some she is a fact which only arises in times of controversy, they regard her from the point of view of convinced opponents. They are certain, whether they have thought out their position or no, that Rome is fundamentally wrong, that, by her extreme view of authority, she has sapped individual responsibility, notably in the Confessional, and has robbed the Gospel of its purity and simplicity by laying stress on unnecessary dogmas and by mediæval superstition. They would say that Rome has lost her spiritual message in her desire for worldly power, and that she is the greatest possible enemy to the soul's free access to its God. Such a point of view of course prevents any close contact with the Catholic Church.

To others she is an ecclesiastical museum—the home of ecclesiastical art, the mother of noble cathedrals whose architecture it is a joy to gaze upon; but she is essentially foreign. So far as they think of her religion they think of it as they, from time to time, have seen it expressed by foreign peoples, and they misunderstand it, think it casual, irreverent, and utterly out of touch with English ways. And so it comes to pass that they wander entranced among the beauties of the Church, yet miss her very soul.

To others, who think more deeply, she is an insoluble enigma. It seems to them as though the Catholic Church should have disappeared from history long ago: they are puzzled at her extraordinary rallying power. Persecuted and turned out of country after country, she still goes on, propped up by the Papal claims which they believe to be utterly false; she has faced more than one apparently overwhelming intellectual revolt, yet still she remains, and they cannot help but admire the amazing unity in which she holds men and women of every nation. But it goes no further, and they explain away this mysterious Church by saying to themselves that the religious instinct is common to all the human race, and exists for all time, and that the Catholic Church is merely the most highly organized expression of that instinct. Their inborn dislike of authority, and their national prejudice against anything foreign, prevent any deeper understanding. And so for them, too, the great secret of the Catholic Church remains unsolved.

Even those who have Catholic friends do not get much further. They accept them as Roman Catholics, and assume that they will observe certain religious duties and refrain from doing certain things which others do. They may, from time to time, be conscious that their Catholic friends understand much more about their religion, and that it means more to them, than is the case with those who belong to the Church of England. But if, for a moment, they are impressed by this, they will say to themselves: "Yes, but it's mainly a religion of fear, fear of the priest who makes excessive use of his authority, and plays upon men and women's sense of duty. Whereas the essence of religion is freedom. Men and women should be free to go to Church because they feel like it and not merely because they are told to."

If there is one section of the English people to-day whom we should expect to understand and have an intimate knowledge of the Catholic Church it would be the Anglo-Catholics. They teach many doctrines in common with her, they read many of her devotional books, and, to a certain extent, they study her theology; yet they are, generally speaking, as far off understanding her as anybody else.

The reason most probably is this—Anglo-Catholics have one absorbing interest, one great, overwhelming longing, and that is the regaining of England for

Our Blessed Lord through the revival of the Catholic Faith in the English Church.

In this great object are centred all their energies, all their prayers, all their sacrifices and all their hopes. They take their stand upon an interpretation of Anglican formularies which has been held by learned and pious men. They are faced with misunderstanding on all sides. They are considered disloyal by many in their own communion, they have to hear their most cherished beliefs denied and often ridiculed by their relatives and their friends. In the past they have been universally persecuted by their bishops, and the bishops to-day, with few exceptions, still do not understand them.

And yet, against overwhelming odds, they have seen their interpretation of the Anglican formularies accepted as a recognized point of view in the Church of England; and many Catholic practices, for which in the past they were persecuted, are now regularly carried out in the services of their Church.

In the midst of this great struggle it is not to be wondered at that they have but little time to think about "Rome." When she does cross their path it is mostly as the great stumbling block to unity. They may, and often do, admire her for having preserved the Faith down the ages; but in their eyes, the dogma of Papal Infallibility has closed the door to that reunion of all Christians within the Catholic Faith, which is the goal of all their hopes. In this reunion they believe the English Church to be the key, the

vital link between the Protestant bodies and Rome.
But, before this can happen, Rome must change
and modify her claims. To most Anglo-Catholics
the Malines discussions were a step in the right
direction, but hopelessly premature. The one thing
is to go on doing the will of Our Blessed Lord where
they are: carrying on the blessed work of the Anglo-
Catholic Revival, leaving the future in the hands of
God. Anglo-Catholics are still fighting with their
backs to the wall, in a fellowship cemented by perse-
cution, misunderstanding and loneliness, and anyone leaving them to join the Roman Church is regarded, even by the most generous and the most
devout, as someone who, if not a traitor, has certainly
let them down and, in some sense, sold the pass.
The way in which anybody who goes over to Rome
is misunderstood is a convincing proof of how little
Anglo-Catholics understand the Catholic Church.

It is almost impossible for Catholics to appreciate
the Anglo-Catholic point of view, and this adds to
the stress of the Anglo-Catholic position, and makes
the leaving of any of their number for the Catholic
Church even harder to bear.

Generally speaking, then, to the average Englishman, the Catholic Church is no more than a name.
For many reasons he is prevented from understanding her. Underneath all other reasons lies the
greatest one of all—the Englishman's love of independence. No interference, least of all in religion or
by a foreigner! Inbred in him, deep set in his sub-

conscious mind, is the instinct that national independence and religious independence go hand in hand. England, he maintains, will never accept an Italian-governed church. If ever he is to come into close and personal touch with the inner life of the Catholic Church, something big must happen—some tremendous jolt in his life—someone he loves dearly must "go over," something must happen to him personally which will shift him beyond national prejudice and personal misunderstanding so that he sees the Catholic Church as she really is.

But, against all this, there is another set of English people—a relatively small but steadily increasing company, by no means confined even mainly to Anglo-Catholics, but representative of all varieties of English life. They are beginning to doubt. Those who are not Anglo-Catholics are conscious of the failure of English religion generally: they are finding it inadequate for their souls' need: they don't know why, but they feel it is all wrong. They are realizing that the Catholic Religion, that religion which four hundred years ago was suppressed by penal laws severer than any other in our national history, is gradually reappearing with a vigour and a strength which they cannot explain on any human reasoning. They see that the great weakness in English religion is its endless sects and controversies, and they are conscious that the Catholics possess a unity unknown in any other society of the world. Their own national prejudices are being weakened by the international spirit moving the world, and they feel the attraction of an international church. They see men and women whom they would least expect to do so becoming members of that Church, and they are wondering and doubting what it all means.

Amongst Anglo-Catholics also there is a little company who are growing anxious. They are beginning to realize that the difference between Anglo-Catholics and Catholics is not merely a matter of detail or degree. They are becoming conscious that Anglo-Catholicism and Catholicism are two quite different things. They see no prospect of reunion. They thought Rome might change, but now they realize she not only will not, but she cannot. The Papacy is fundamental, the very basis of all her authority and her unity. They see that, so far from the Catholic Church ever contemplating reunion, she is spending herself lavishly in money and in men, is building her own cathedrals, her churches and her schools, and gradually becoming the greatest religious force in the country.

This company of doubting and wondering souls has increased rapidly of late, and there is every sign that it will increase more rapidly in the future.

But to me, as I stood in that autumn of 1924 with the autobiography of St. Thérèse in my hand, these doubts and wonderings had not as yet occurred. I was entirely absorbed in the conversion of souls to Our Blessed Lord through the Anglo-Catholic

revival in the English Church. I had no sense
whatever of insecurity, no doubts whatever as to
my position. It was not till another year and a half
had passed that I was to experience the beginnings
of those torturing doubts and that sickening sense of
fear that was gradually to fill my mind. The tremendous "jolt" had not come to me; it was to come at
Lisieux, but not till eighteen months had passed.

I took the *Life of St. Thérèse* up to my room and
began to read it. The first two chapters did not
appeal to me at all: indeed, I found it difficult to get
through them. Gradually, however, the story
gripped me, and it is quite impossible to describe
my state of mind when at last, long after midnight,
I laid down the book. All I can say is that it moved
my whole being as no other piece of writing has
ever done.

Here was someone who had loved Our Lord to a
degree beyond anything I had met before: a love as
strong as that of the martyrs of old, and yet with the
delicacy and tenderness of a little child, so delicate
and tender that one almost fails to realize the furnace
in which that love was so wonderfully refined.
Above all else it was the Saint's gospel of suffering
as being the most blessed gift by which alone we
could be really united to Our Blessed Lord in un-
fettered love, and her interpretation of pain and
suffering as something which can be offered in
union with Our Blessed Lord's Cross for the sake

of the Church and for the salvation of souls—it was all this which, coming into my life when things were exceedingly difficult, lit up and made real to me eertain spiritual truths towards which I was dimly groping; truths which I had been discouraged from holding as being morbid and so forth, and which I now found were the very foundations of the saintly life. For the first time I understood St. Paul's words—"I fill up that which is behind of the afflictions of Christ in my flesh for His Body's sake, which is the Church" (COL. i, 24).

For over six months the study of this book pulled me through one of the most difficult passages of my life.

CHAP. II : *FIRST VISIT TO LISIEUX*

In the following May, soon after Easter, I was given the annual three weeks rest which is usual in the brotherhood to which I then belonged. A few days before my rest was due it was suggested to me by my sister that I should go on a short pilgrimage to Lisieux, and visit the home and Convent where St. Thérèse had lived. The whole thing was decided upon only at the very last moment. I naturally shrank from the journey, for I knew if I went to Lisieux I must go entirely alone, and I had never been in France before and had never spoken French since my school-days. It was all I could do to get my passport ready in time. I so very nearly did not go at all. But I went. At Havre, where the boat arrived in the early morning, I attended Mass at one of the churches. After the Mass an old priest shuffled round the church with two acolytes and a crucifix and the funniest old beadle with a cocked hat and staff in front, all of them chanting a litany in some foreign tongue. It was all so casual and offhand. I remember saying to myself: "Well, if that is Roman Catholicism, I'm glad I'm not an R.C."

The train wound its way through a lovely valley, from the window I saw the little Normandy

farms, with their orchards and apple blossom. As
the train approached Lisieux I could see the Basilica
of the Convent; within whose walls the Saint had
prayed and loved and suffered. The moment when
I looked upon it for the first time is a moment of
my life which it is impossible to forget.

Arrived at Lisieux, I made my way to the hotel,
small and primitive, and then set out for the Chapel
of the Convent where is the Shrine of the little
Saint. My first impression was one of great repulsion:
it was all so foreign, sentimental and artificial. I
couldn't bear the paper flowers, the festoons of paper
roses. I did not learn till later in the day that these
were in honour of the Canonization of the Saint
which was then taking place at Rome. All un-
knowingly I had stumbled upon the very day of her
Canonization for my first visit to her shrine. I
made my way through crowds of people to the
Shrine, which also did not appeal to me, said my
prayers, and came away.

In the afternoon I visited the Hall of the Relics.
There I saw various things which the Saint had
either worn or used: the spoon and fork used by her
in the refectory, the habits she had worn, her needle
case, her sandals, the chair and table which she had
used in her cell, the pictures she had painted, little
artificial flowers which she had made as she lay
dying, and, above all, her discipline of knotted
cord and other methods of mortification which she
had used.

It was a most moving experience to be looking upon the very things used by one who in so short a time had been raised to the Altars of the Church and was now proclaimed a Saint in every country of the world; to be treading the very streets which she had trod—trod in our own lifetime, too.

Later in the afternoon I visited her home, a charming little house set in the middle of the garden where St. Thérèse, as a child, had played. In this garden I saw the little alcove in the wall where she placed her baby altar and, at Christmas, her baby crib; the very figures which she used can still be seen. I entered the house by the room near the fireplace of which she used to place her shoes on Christmas Eve, as English children hang their stockings by their beds, and I remembered that memorable night when she did it for the last time.

Opening out of this room is another which can only be seen through a glass door. This is the room where the family had their last meal before the Saint entered the convent. In this room also is the chair in which her father used to sit and sing to her, and the little footstool on which, as a small child, she sat at her father's feet.

Upstairs is the room in which she was so desperately ill, and where she saw Our Lady's miraculous smile. In the place where her bed used to be, there is now an Altar. Finally, in another room, one is shown all her toys, her school satchel and exercise books; her prayer desk and rosary and catechism, all kept carefully behind glass doors.

The contrast between the toys of the frail child and the discipline of the strong and full grown Saint was deeply moving, a perfect parable of the power of Divine Grace.

On my way back I visited the Cathedral of St. Pierre, and saw the Altar where the family all made their last Communion together before the Convent received the Saint within its walls. Behind the High Altar is the perfect Lady Chapel which Cauchon, Bishop of Beauvais, who condemned St. Joan, built as an act of reparation. At this Altar St. Thérèse used to hear her daily Mass as a girl. I summoned up courage to ask an old verger, in very broken French, if he knew the Saint personally; and he told me that he remembered her and her father very well, and that he had often received money from her.

That evening, after I had had dinner in the most obscure corner I could find, the landlady, noticing I was alone, came and talked with me for a while. She told me she used to be in the same class as St. Thérèse in the Convent school and had often sat next her in form.

So ended the first day at Lisieux, a day crowded with vivid and deep impressions, an increasing consciousness of the Supernatural and a growing sense of the nearness of the Unseen and the Saints.

The following day I was present at Mass at the

Shrine of the Saint. I again found the foreign atmosphere very difficult and could not get used to their ways at all.

In the afternoon I paid another visit to the little home of St. Thérèse, intending to read quietly in the garden. While I was reading a Belgian priest came and sat beside me and we talked for a while as best we could, for my French was very meagre. I remember the subjects of our talk were the harassing questions of Divorce and Birth Control. On rising to go we found that, being Ascension Day, the house was closed an hour earlier than usual, and the garden door was locked and barred. "Nous sommes les prisonniers de la petite Thérèse," exclaimed the Belgian priest, in great excitement. We examined the wall in vain, there was no possibility of climbing over. "Je vais chercher une échelle," said my stout little friend. By a stroke of great good luck we found the needed ladder in the toolhouse at the end of the garden, and we propped it up against the wall. But once again we were foiled, for there was nobody to whom we could appeal for help upon the other side. So my companion and I found an old tin can, in which he placed a stone and, sitting astraddle the wall, he rattled it for all he was worth. Presently neighbours began to gather round; whereupon my little companion, seated astride the wall, and waving the old tin can, shouted out at the top of his voice "Nous sommes prisonniers de la petite Thérèse, nous deux, un prêtre belge et un anglais! Vive l'Alliance!" Meanwhile I was cowering at the foot of the wall, terribly shy and dreading a public scene in a foreign land: finally I climbed the wall, amid great applause, and reached the ground and freedom.

It was a terribly funny incident, but its consequences were to be of far more importance than I then imagined. In consequence of the delay I arrived at the hotel late for dinner, to find the dining room flooded out with pilgrims from Rome. I was thus forced out of my solitary corner to the very middle of the room, where was the only vacant seat left. I found myself opposite an Irishman from Glasgow. He immediately got into conversation with me, and asked me to go with him on the following morning to visit the Convent cemetery and see the place where St. Thérèse had originally been buried. I replied that I was not very interested, as her body was no longer there, having been removed to the Convent Chapel. He pressed me, however, and at last I consented to go.

The way to the cemetery lies along a most lovely country lane. The over-arching trees were of a fresh young green, and spring flowers were coming up everywhere. The distant view across the valley is exquisite. It is the path along which the Saint had often passed to lay flowers on her mother's grave. We paused at this grave and said a prayer and then passed on to the Convent cemetery.

While we were there a French lady began to speak to us about the Saint and her life. She pointed

to the graves near by and said this was the Reverend
Mother who received St. Thérèse into the Convent—
this was her first novice mistress, and so forth.
Seeing that she possessed intimate knowledge of the
Convent, I asked her to tell me anything she knew
about St. Thérèse. . . .

We returned to the town, accompanied by this
French lady and her husband. On the way I explained to her, as I already had to my Irish companion, that I was an Anglo-Catholic. She was
greatly puzzled and much interested, and said that,
if I was willing, she would try and get me a private
audience with the Reverend Mother of the Carmelite Convent, Mère Agnes, the elder sister of St.
Thérèse. She said she feared it was not very likely,
but that she would try.

We arranged to meet at a certain point an hour
later. At the appointed time I was there waiting;
but there was no sign of her. I had just abandoned
hope and was moving off when she appeared. We
had made a mistake about our rendezvous, and I
very nearly missed the interview altogether. She
told me she had secured an appointment, and off we
went together, she acting as interpreter.

And so it came to pass that I, a complete stranger,
of a different Communion, knowing nobody, and
scarcely able to make myself understood, found
myself kneeling in the little parlour of the Carmelite
Convent, speaking with Mère Agnes—Pauline—
the elder sister of St. Thérèse, kneeling where, years

before, St. Thérèse had knelt in floods of tears, talking to the same sister, "her little Mother Pauline"—listening to the same voice—after her entrance to the Convent. The interview was very short, and we spoke at the grille, with a white curtain in between. The only word I can recall is the word "abjurer," when I was told I must renounce all my false beliefs. I remember saying to myself: "Yes, that is exactly what she would say, because she understands nothing of the Catholic revival in the English Church."

Outside we met the Curé, with whom I had a short conversation. He asked me what my authority was. I replied quite cheerfully "the universal episcopate," whereupon he said, "Mais où est-il?" I remember that I could make no convincing answer but consoled myself with the thought that it was safer to be too vague rather than too definite.

The following morning I spent my last few hours in Lisieux. I paid a short visit to the Benedictine school where the Saint had been educated, and saw the Altar where she was confirmed and made her first Communion.

I then made a last visit to the little home of St. Thérèse to say a final prayer. As I entered, the Sister-in-Charge came forward and asked if I were a Catholic. I explained that I was an Anglo-Catholic. She was much interested, and then said "I want to give you a special favour." With that she unlocked the glass door, and I was allowed to enter and kneel and say a prayer at the table where the Saint had had her last meal and to kiss the little footstool upon which she had sat. The sister took me to the other room and again opened the glass door, and I was allowed to hold the Saint's skipping-rope in my hand and kneel at her prayer-desk and kiss her catechism —a privilege the sister told me she had given to scarcely anybody.

I then had to hurry to catch my train, and my three days visit to Lisieux was over. At Trouville I had to wait, and I spent the time on the beach where St. Thérèse first saw the sea—and there I thought out the experience of those three days.

Standing out far above all else was the fact that I had been through a spiritual experience unlike anything I had ever known in my life before. Putting aside the novelty of it all, the beauty of the old town of Lisieux, its exquisite setting in the loveliness of a Normandy spring, and allowing for the fact that the Saint had died in the attractiveness of her youth, I still knew that I had been in the presence of the Supernatural as never before. The expression which the Supernatural had taken and through which it had made itself real to me was the life of St. Thérèse, a life of love for Our Blessed Lord so absolute, so complete and so consuming that it defied all human analysis and exceeded all human understanding. So stern in its renunciation that it made one afraid, yet so simple and so human in its homeliness that one was utterly unable to resist it.

It seemed to vanquish time and transcend all human
ties. Earth and earthly things only counted in so
far as they were in tune with Our Lord's Love for
her and with her absorbing love for Him.

It was the quality of love which one had read of
in the Lives of the Saints, and which one had wist-
fully regarded as a thing of the past. It took one
straight back to the Colosseum at Rome. Here it was
to-day, the same invincible supernatural love of the
early martyrs, the same heroic sanctity—in our own
time, in the midst of this most material age. A
Supernatural love which revealed with an intensity
which I had never met before, the true relation of the
individual to Our Blessed Lord; the relation of the
creature to its Creator, the soul to its God. That is,
a relationship of utter adoration and worship, and
yet at the same time of perfect union of the soul with
its Saviour. Any question and doubt as to the Godhead of Our Lord Jesus Christ was impossible at
Lisieux. All the wearying discussions in which Our
Lord is regarded as the Great Example Who
encourages us to develop the God within us were
unthinkable. The Deity of Christ was flashed
before my soul at Lisieux with blinding splendour.
My soul drank at the pure stream of the undiluted
truth of the Godhead of My Lord.

I had known it through the reading of her Life
and my soul had fed upon it, yet I had rather felt she
was not of this world. But here at Lisieux was the
house in which she had lived, the toys with which

he had played, the things she had used and worn,
he very street along which she had walked, and all
his had happened within our very lifetime.

The reason why I lingered among the earthly
relics of the Saint was not out of mere sentimentality,
as some readers may be inclined to think, but because they were the pledge that this saintly soul was
also very human—not merely a saintly tradition, but
human here with us in our very day. And, as I saw
them, I knew that the days of heroic sanctity were
not over, a miracle of Supernatural Grace was
before my eyes.

It was because I had read her life of unquenchable
love for Our Blessed Lord, radiant through the
greatest sufferings, physical and spiritual, and
through a very painful death, that these little earthly
tokens were so very precious to me.

By the power of her life and love, I had been
caught up so that I had been nearer to Our
Blessed Lord and had seen Him more clearly. The
simple directness of her love had made the Object
of that love seem very, very close. Love radiated
from her shrine and gathered into a Supernatural
fellowship those who knelt around. I had been
where the Unseen was very, very near, and where
the veil was very, very thin.

The second great fact of which I was conscious
was that my visit was being guided in a mysterious
way. One after the other barriers were broken
down and hindrances removed without any attempt

to do so on my part. At first it seemed coincidence, and some may so interpret it even now; but as time went on I knew it was more than mere coincidence which had led me, a stranger and all unknown, to kneel in the Carmel parlour and receive the blessing of Mère Agnes, the Saint's own sister. I must believe it was the prayers of the little Saint herself.

At the same time, had I not read her Life before I went, I never should have got over the many superficial hindrances which so put me off, the foreign ways which I so disliked: and I can quite understand English people going to Lisieux and coming away without ever having learnt its secret.

The Catholic Church, as such, did not greatly attract me. I was merely conscious of an astounding spiritual experience for which I was intensely grateful to Our Blessed Lord. It did not give me any desire to become a Catholic or any thought that I should do so: on the contrary when, returning on the boat, I read in the paper of some incomprehensibly uncharitable statement by a certain Anglican Bishop concerning the Blessed Sacrament, it merely made me long for the day when all that I had seen at Lisieux, the devotion to Our Saviour in the Blessed Sacrament, would be the very life and breath of the Church of England. It made me resolve more than ever to spend myself to that great end.

So I returned to my ministry, intending, if I could, to return to Lisieux another year.

CHAP. III : *SECOND VISIT*

THE year passed quickly, filled with active ministry of every description: the experience of Lisieux always at the back of my mind. To this experience I returned continually to refresh my soul. At times I had vague misgivings as to why I had never met anything like it in the Church of England, but I met them quite easily with the answer that it was only a matter of time, and, with the growth of Anglo-Catholicism, the same thing would be possible in the Church of England. We were rebuilding the waste places, and that was sufficient for me! Mainly, my attitude was one of great gratitude for having been allowed such an experience and a desire to test its reality by a second visit.

And so, in the following May of 1926, I paid my second visit. The scene was the same. Outwardly everything was just as before, and yet everything was different. The Saint had retired entirely into the background—and I found my whole mind focussed not on the Saint herself, but upon one all-absorbing point—"What was it that had made such a life possible? What was it that had produced Thérèse?"

Hitherto I had always taken it for granted that it

was the personal Faith of the Saint and her complete response to Our Lord and His Divine Will, even in the darkest moments. But now I had to ask myself what I meant by the word Faith. Brought up in Anglicanism, with its inevitable vagueness and its fear of precise definition in spiritual things, I had never defined it. So far as I had thought it out, it meant to me the capacity to believe in certain spiritual truths which, though I could not prove them, were not contrary to my reason; a capacity to cling on to one's belief in the goodness of God and the ultimate triumph of truth in the midst of confusion in matters of belief, and to cling on to Christian standards in the midst of overwhelming difficulties in the question of morals.

But here, in the case of St. Thérèse, I knew I was faced with something quite different, something far more definite and of far greater force. She had indeed the capacity to cling on by Faith in the darkest moments and to believe things beyond her reason; but she had all this in a unique degree because, behind and beneath it all, was a supernatural certainty in those Divine truths which she knew had been revealed and which she never for one moment doubted or questioned. These truths she did not question: not because her reason led her to believe in them, but because they were taught by an authority outside her which she knew to possess a divinely given authority which could never err or contradict itself in matters of faith. And it was because she was resting on this foundation that, free from endless controversies, her soul was able to grow and develop in such a marvellous way.

I had always regarded such certainty in matters of Faith as something impossible in this world and not even to be desired; because it could only be achieved at the expense of character and intellect, and by crippling all sincerity and growth; held that thinking things out for oneself was the condition of character.

And yet here I was faced with the fact that it was precisely this certainty coming to St. Thérèse from an objective authority outside her which had produced the most intelligently saintly life I had known.

But more than this, St. Thérèse did not possess the certainty by herself alone; it was shared by every individual within her Church. This was one of the facts, I began to see, which had given Lisieux its astounding spiritual quality. At Lisieux were gathered people of all nations from every part of the world, all perfectly at ease with one another because perfectly one in their belief. Such a unity in matters of Faith among people from all parts of the world, I was gradually learning, could not be of man's devising. It was not that each one had worked out his own idea of the Christian Religion, and that they had all happened to agree, but it was because they all believed in a definite authority which they knew to be supernatural and divine, to which they gave an unhesitating and loving obedience. And this authority was not a crippling, mutilating thing, but was creative and productive in the highest degree possible.

I began to see that to me Faith was mainly the result of my own reason. I accepted what I could not prove, provided it did not contradict my reasoning.

Whereas to St. Thérèse Faith was belief in certain truths because they had been revealed to and taught by a Teacher outside her which had divine authority and therefore the right to claim her absolute obedience.

To me the centre of Faith lay in myself. To her it lay in the Church. To me, according to the theories I held then, her view of Faith seemed rather irrational, and yet, with Lisieux before me, I knew it was not so.

I had not as yet realized the close relationship between reason and authority; that it is the function of reason to guide us to where the divine authority rests, and that the authority itself must be able to meet the challenge of reason, one of God's greatest gifts to man, or else cease to exist, for only truth can prevail.

But at the moment I was only dimly groping towards the Catholic definition of Faith: "Faith is a supernatural gift of God which enables us to believe without doubting whatever God has revealed."

"Whatever God has revealed."

Where was God's revelation to be found, and where was the authority empowered to carry out the gigantic trust of guarding this revelation and teaching it to humanity all down the ages? Where lay the source of this authority, calling for such supernatural obedience? Where was the centre of this supernatural unity? There was only one answer. At last, for the first time in my life, I found myself face to face with the Papacy as the greatest spiritual force in human life. Hitherto I had never examined the Papal claims closely. I regarded it as indeed a great power, but a power mainly of human contrivance. Rome had been the centre of the world, and had gradually assumed the control of ecclesiastical affairs. Temporal power and astute diplomacy at the Vatican had slowly built up an invincible position, often by very questionable methods. Some nations had had the courage to assert their spiritual independence, and nearly half the Christian world rejected the Papal claims. And there I had left it.

But now I realized that such an immense body as the Catholic Church could not be kept together, human nature being what it is, unless the centre of unity was of divine origin. And now I began to see a further fact; namely, that this inner unity of Faith was the secret of the wonderful external and visible unity of the Catholic Church. I had always suspected the outward unity of the Catholic Church as an unreal superficial unity forced upon people by authority from above, an iron system silencing all original thought, shutting out light and air, a system in which the individual was completely crushed—a unity of organization and not of spirit. I now knew that I could no longer so easily believe this. At Lisieux it was shown to me clearly that the secret of the external unity was to be found in the spiritual unity of the Faith. The more I thought about this the more obvious it became that the marvellous external unity of the Catholic Church, holding in one absolute obedience souls from every quarter of the world, could never have come about, still less existed longer than any other kingdom, on any foundation which was not supernatural and divine. The Catholic Church was one because her Faith was one, nor could the unity of the Faith be preserved in the face of the independence of the human intellect unless the authority was divine.

Again, the fact that at least half the Christian world accepted this authority and jealously guarded this unity was, I could see, far more impressive than the other half, which had split up into endless sects, at war not only with the Catholic Church, but with one another.

For a week I pondered these questions in my mind in the lanes and fields round Lisieux and argued this way and that, but in the end I knew that I could

never again rest until this question of authority
and unity had been settled.

Did Our Blessed Lord intend His Church to be a
teaching church, possessing this absolute authority,
teaching one Faith, and demanding this complete
obedience from men? Did He intend that His
Church should be visibly one? And did He mean
that St. Peter and his successors were to be the
final authority and the centre of unity for His
Church?

I knew I could not be honest unless I faced this
question. I shrank from it with all my being, for, if
the Roman Catholic claim proved to be right, I
knew that every step I took was bound to tear my
whole life up by the roots, destroy my apparent
usefulness, cause endless pain and dismay to many
souls whom I loved more dearly than words could
say, and lead me right out into loneliness and the fear
of the unknown.

But at that moment I was not at all convinced, and
did not think it could be possible that Our Lord
could claim such an upheaval. All I knew at the
moment was that I had got to study and read my
New Testament over again with these three questions foremost in my mind—Authority—Unity—
Peter.

I cannot describe the sense of loneliness and helplessness with which I left Lisieux this second time.
Helplessness, for I was ill equipped for such a

gigantic task upon which so many issues hung, and loneliness because nothing is more misunderstood by even the closest of friends than "serious Roman difficulties."

And so, with a very anxious heart, I turned to my New Testament, and the next part contains the story of what I found there.

PART II

PART II

CHAP. IV : *AUTHORITY IN THE NEW TESTAMENT*

To the average Englishman the question of any authority in his religion hardly ever occurs. He accepts that aspect of the Church of England's teaching in which he has been brought up, either Anglo-Catholic, Broad, or Evangelical, and follows it until it either fails to satisfy his needs or else comes into conflict with his own personal views about God and Religion.

He then, being essentially honest and sincere and not desiring to profess more than he really believes, discards all that he cannot accept and evolves a personal religion of his own.

About this religion, so formed, he is intensely reserved, and, if questioned about it, he would say with complete conviction that religion to him was a matter entirely between God and the soul, that each man must find it out for himself and do his best to live up to it, that, if he had to label himself, he was of course Church of England, but that he did not wish to ally himself with any particular party and would always treat all religion with respect. In taking up this attitude he would be extremely modest and diffident.

But the moment there is any suggestion of an ecclesiastical Authority which has the power to guide a man's religion and to say quite definitely what he ought or ought not to believe, and what he ought or ought not to do, an authority which at times will make demands upon him which will be against his own personal judgments, then at once he becomes restive and anxious.

He is filled with very definite fears of being asked to surrender his independence of conscience to another man, and he tells himself how grossly the power of the Priesthood was abused in mediæval times. He also feels subconsciously that all this fear is bound up with that sturdy independence which is the characteristic of the English nation and has been the source of its greatness; and, if pressed beyond a certain limit, the modest and diffident Englishman will put up the stiffest fight possible for his independence in religion. He will do this not because he desires a fight but because of his deepest conviction that that independence, which he prizes above all else in national affairs, is ever more vital in things which concern a man's soul. Without this independence men become partizans narrow followers of narrow sects, intolerant and controversial, and lose that liberality of outlook which is specially English and specially needed in these modern times.

This attitude of mind is strengthened by the fact that amongst an increasing number of men there is a growing doubt at the back of their minds as to whether the Gospels are really reliable; whether the Christian religion is authoritative for all the world; and whether we can really know what Our Lord's teaching actually was. They would hesitate before saying that they believed Our Lord to be truly God. To them Jesus Christ is the great, broad-minded teacher, basing everything on the love of God and the love of our fellow-men. What more could you want? To be more definite is dangerous.

In this atmosphere it is obvious that Authority can have no real place. Where all is so vague nobody can claim to speak with authority.

Now this shrinking from any definite ecclesiastical Authority pervades all religion in the Church of England to-day. In Evangelical and Broad Church circles it is obvious, but it also exists among the Anglo-Catholics, who sincerely desire a measure of Church Authority. For their desire is mainly for an authority which will give a backing to certain doctrines, which by their individual intellect and judgment they have come to accept. Therefore, if that authority should conflict at any point with that judgment and intellect, it would cease to have any weight. Such a view of authority leaves room for independence and private judgment. But Catholics accept the authority of the Church because they believe it to be divinely ordained authority to which they give absolute submission; knowing that even in those doctrines which seem unacceptable to their intellect and judgment, the Church will in the end be found to be right, because she is the Divinely ordained teacher of truth. This view of authority leaves no room for private judgment. It was not until I came face to face with the Authority of the Catholic Church as I saw it at Lisieux; absolute and unbending, demanding in the Name of Our Lord a complete submission of the individual; it was not till then that I realized how different this was from the Anglo-Catholic conception.

I found myself recoiling from it, filled with doubts and fears. Surely such an extreme view of authority was unnecessary, crippling to human intellect and social progress: surely it meant the suicide of individuality. Above all, surely this was utterly unlike the Mind of Our Blessed Lord in the Gospels, and yet I could not get away from the conviction that there was something supernatural in this Authority, though I distrusted and feared it so much.

And so in this frame of mind I turned to the Gospels; hardly believing that they could support this view of authority; and yet half fearing that they might.

CHAP. V : *THE AUTHORITY OF OUR LORD IN THE GOSPELS*

In turning to the Gospels to see what they taught about Authority, I found that, so far from being vague and undefined, it was most clear and most decided. If we turn to St. Matthew, St. Mark and St. Luke we find that it runs throughout them all.

At the very opening of His ministry Our Blessed Lord is shown to us as a Person Who teaches with a unique authority:

"And it came to pass when Jesus had ended these sayings the people were astonished at His doctrine for He taught them as one having authority and not as the Scribes" (MATT. vii, 28, 29).

"And they were all amazed, insomuch that they questioned among themselves saying What thing is this? What new doctrine is this? For with authority commandeth He even the unclean spirits and they do obey Him" (MARK i, 27).

"And they were astonished at His doctrine, for His word was with power" (LUKE iv, 32).

"And many hearing Him were astonished saying From whence hath this Man these things? And what wisdom is this which is given unto Him?" (MARK vi, 2).

With His own lips Our Blessed Lord claims that this authority is greater than all that has gone before; and that it is supernatural and eternal:

"It was said by them of old time . . . . but I say unto you" (MATT. v, 21).

"Heaven and earth shall pass away but My Words shall not pass away" (MATT. xxiv, 35).

No wonder that His enemies were afraid of Him and dared not question Him:

"They feared Him, because all the people was astonished at His doctrine" (MARK xi, 18).

"No man after that durst ask Him any question" (MARK xii, 34).

So definite was the authority with which Our Lord spoke and acted that it drove His enemies to a direct challenge. The chief priests asked Him 'By what authority doest Thou these things, and who gave Thee this authority?"

Finally Our Lord Himself, with His own lips, claims absolute and complete authority both in Heaven and Earth:

"All authority is given unto Me in Heaven and in Earth" (MATT. xxviii, 18). "All things are delivered to Me of My Father" (LUKE x, 22).

In these passages we see Our Blessed Lord as Someone Who speaks with an authority unlike any other, an authority so clear and definite that everybody recognized it. His friends marvelled at it; His enemies were driven to challenge it and were reduced to silence and fear, being utterly unable to answer Him. Lastly, Our Blessed Lord claims for His words a permanence which extends beyond time and space, and deliberately tells us that He possesses all authority, not only on earth but in Heaven as well.

When we turn to St. John's Gospel, the evidence is even clearer. Our Lord definitely claims that this authority comes direct from God the Father:

"I proceeded forth and came from God; neither came I of Myself but He sent Me" (JOHN viii, 42).

"My doctrine is not Mine, but His that sent Me" (John vii, 16).

"He Whom God hath sent speaketh the words of God, for God giveth not the spirit by measure unto him. The Father loveth the Son and hath given all things into His Hand" (St. John iii, 34).

"The Father judgeth no man but hath committed all judgment unto the Son" (JOHN v, 22).

And because His teaching comes from God the Father, therefore it is the Truth:

"But now ye seek to kill Me, a Man that hath told you the truth, which I have heard of God" (JOHN viii, 40).

"If ye continue in My Word, then are ye My disciples indeed, and ye shall know the truth, and the truth shall make you free" (JOHN viii, 31).

In the final discourses before the Passion, spoken to His twelve Apostles, He states deliberately, "I am the Truth" (John XIV, 6).

Above all, in order it seems that there should be no possible mistake, He makes this claim again before Pilate at one of the most crucial moments of the Passion:

"For this cause came I into the world that I should bear witness unto the Truth" (JOHN xviii, 37).

Thus the Gospel picture of Our Lord is not merely the picture of One Who loved all men with a Love greater than any other love this world has ever seen, but of One Who also spoke with a unique Authority, claiming to be a Teacher of a Divine revelation given Him from God the Father, a revelation which therefore all men must listen to and obey because it is the Truth. Heaven and Earth may pass, but His teaching will remain because it is the Truth.

Our Lord always taught that the true love of humanity must always go hand in hand with an answering love of truth. The two things in fact are the same; and indeed it must be so, for love which is not founded on truth is merely sentimentalism and weakness, lacking that element of sacrifice and surrender without which it is not love, but self-indulgence.

Let us now face this. We are confronted with the most overwhelming fact in the history of the human race—God Himself has, as a matter of history, come down to earth—not just a great teacher or a great prophet, but God Himself, in the Person of Jesus Christ, has lived amongst men. Why? In order to reveal to mankind the Truth about God and the Truth about mankind—and to show man the method of his salvation.

When Our Lord Jesus Christ speaks it is God speaking. It follows then that His teaching is the whole Truth and carries with it the whole Authority of God. This teaching clearly can never change, for Truth cannot contradict itself. It cannot belong to any one people alone; it belongs to the whole of the human race. When God speaks the whole of mankind must listen and obey. If a man comes face to face with this Divine Teacher and wilfully rejects His teaching, he is condemned.

And yet this Teacher is no mere arbitrary Judge. He is the greatest Lover of humanity the world has ever known. He has held the heart of the world captive ever since He came amongst men.

But His love is not a weak, sentimental love, giving way to human weakness, but a strong and vigorous love. And when men wanted it to be untrue to Truth, it gave itself by dying for the Truth; as all real Love must, for Love and Truth can never be opposed.

The most perfect revelation of Truth is the Divine Love dying for Truth's sake on the Cross.

But at this point someone may very fairly say: "If this is true, we are faced with a gigantic fact; but how do we know that the Gospels are a reliable record? May not the Evangelists or the translators have made mistakes, can we be really sure of what Our Lord actually did say?"

The next chapter will be devoted to the answer to this question. At the moment all we will say is that the Gospels depend for their authority upon the authority of the Society which produced them. If the Scripture records are true and inspired, it is because the original Christian Society, the Catholic Church, which drew them up and sanctioned their publication, was herself divinely inspired and had Divine Authority to do so.

And this Catholic Church, by her tradition and teaching, has always taught, from the very earliest times, that Jesus of Nazareth is God and Man—a truth which she has enshrined for ever in her Creeds.

"Jesus Christ, The Only Begotten Son of God, begotten of His Father before all worlds . . . . Very God of Very God, Begotten, not made. Being of one Substance with the Father, by Whom all things were made. Who for us men . . . came down from Heaven . . . . and was made Man."

CHAP. VI : *THE AUTHORITY OF THE CHURCH IN THE GOSPELS*

How are we to know whether all this is true? We have seen in the Gospel record that Our Blessed Lord is both God and Man—Perfect God and Perfect Man. When Our Lord speaks, it is God speaking. When He teaches, it is the whole Truth; and His teaching carries with it the whole Authority of God, and those who hear must obey it. He clearly claimed to be God; this claim was recognized by foes and friends alike. He was put to death because of this claim, and He rose from the grave to prove His claim to be true. But how are we to know that this gigantic thing has really happened? Before we accept such a tremendous fact we must be sure of our ground. How are we to know that the Gospel narratives are correct? Did Our Lord really make this claim? Are the teachings recorded in the Gospels really true? The Gospels were written some years after He had left this world. What happened in between? Did Our Lord's Authority cease when He ascended or did He leave some means by which it should be continued down the ages? If so, where is it? The reliability of the Gospels must depend upon some such authority.

Let us examine the Gospels once more. In them we find that Our Lord had handed His Authority on to His Apostles, who were to be the founders of His Church, and that Church was to be the shrine of His Divine Authority to the end of time. Let us look at the passages in which Our Lord gives this great Commission to His Church. Each Gospel records this Commission:

"All power is given unto Me in heaven and in earth. Go ye therefore and teach all nations . . . . teaching them to observe all things whatsoever I have commanded you: and, lo, I am with you alway, even unto the end of the world" (MATT. xxviii, 18).

"Go ye into all the world, and preach the gospel to every creature. He that believeth and is baptised shall be saved: but he that believeth not shall be condemned" (MARK xvi, 15).

"Behold I send the promise of My Father upon you: but tarry ye in the city of Jerusalem until ye be endued with power from on high" (LUKE xxiv, 49).

"As My Father hath sent Me, even so send I you. And when He had said this He breathed on them and saith unto them: Receive ye the Holy Ghost. Whose so ever sins ye remit they are remitted unto them and whose so ever sins ye retain they are retained" (JOHN xx, 21).

Here we see that the Church is sent forth into the world with an authority Supernatural and Divine; an authority which is absolute, and which flows from Our Blessed Lord Himself, Who is Supreme in heaven and in earth. "All power is given unto Me in heaven and in earth. Go ye therefore."

Our Lord sends His Church with a Mission which He identifies with nothing less than the Mission with which He Himself had been sent into the world by the Father. "As My Father hath sent Me, even so send I you." Could anything be clearer, more solemn, or more direct? Our Lord goes on to make it perfectly clear what this Mission is; it is nothing less than to teach to the whole world the whole Truth as He had taught it to them.—"Go ye and teach all nations . . . teaching them to observe all things whatsoever I have commanded you." "Go ye into all the world and preach the Gospel to every creature."

Think for a moment of the immensity of the task— A little company of uneducated and ignorant Jews, men who had hardly been outside their own country, entrusted with the teaching of the Supreme Revelation of God to Man; and this Revelation they are to teach to the whole world. They will have to meet the varying temperaments of the different nations and learn their languages; and they will have to commend their Gospel to the great philosophers of Athens, Corinth and Rome.

It is a task clearly quite impossible and utterly

beyond their powers; unless they are given some supernatural guidance which shall protect them from any fundamental error; and unless they know that they possess this supernatural guidance. How else could they have confidence to teach, and how else would anybody be won to accept their teaching?

This supernatural guidance Our Blessed Lord promised on two occasions. One occasion was when He gave them their great Commission, in St. Matthew's Gospel, and ended by promising them His protecting and guiding Presence till the end of the world. "Lo, I am with you alway, even unto the end of the world."

The second occasion was during the solemn discourse to His Apostles after the Last Supper:

"I will pray The Father and He shall give you another Comforter, that He may abide with you for ever; even the Spirit of Truth" (JOHN xiv, 16).

"The Holy Ghost, Whom the Father will send in My Name, He shall teach you all things, and bring all things to your remembrance, whatsoever I have said unto you" (JOHN xiv, 26).

"When He, the Spirit of Truth, is come, He will guide you into all truth" (JOHN xvi, 13).

This promise, which He had made in the discourse after the Last Supper, He repeated in the most dramatic manner and with the utmost emphasis just before His Ascension, when He said to His Apostles:

"Behold I send the promise of My Father upon you, but tarry ye in the city of Jerusalem until ye be endued with power from on high" (LUKE xxiv, 49.)

It is difficult to see how Our Lord could have been more definite or more precise on this great point. If Christianity is the Revelation of God, committed to human men to teach and to guard till the end of time in the face of human nature as we know it, it seems that some such infallible guidance is essential.

That this infallibility, this protection from error, was given to the Apostles by Our Lord is doubly proved by Our Lord's terrific words in St. Mark:

"Go ye into all the world and preach the Gospel to every creature. He that believeth . . . . shall be saved, but he that believeth not *shall be condemned*."

What Society can dare to say that anyone who believes its teaching will be saved and that anyone who wilfully disbelieves will be condemned unless that Society is certain that it has a Divine Revelation committed to its charge by God Himself, and that it has been given an infallible guidance in the teaching of it? Again, what power would such a Society's condemnation carry if men did not realize that it was divinely guided?

So far, then, the Gospel records tell us that Our Lord committed all His Authority to His Apostles, commanded them to teach the whole Truth to the whole world, and promised that He would protect them from all error to the end of time: so that they should command the obedience of men, and so that all who wilfully destroyed their authority would be condemned.

And this Authority, though definite, was not to be inconsistent with the highest possible degree of love. In the discourse after the Last Supper, St. John tells us how Our Lord, Who gave such authority to His Church, commanded them with the greatest earnestness to love one another as He had loved them:

"As the Father hath loved Me, so have I loved you: continue ye in My Love" (JOHN xv, 9).

"This is My Commandment, that ye love one another as I have loved you" (JOHN xv, 12).

"Greater love hath no man than this, that a man lay down his life for his friends" (JOHN xv, 13).

"A new Commandment I give unto you, that ye love one another: as I have loved you, that ye also love one another. By this shall all men know that ye are My disciples, if ye have love one to another" (JOHN xiii, 34).

Love and Authority go hand in hand in the

Gospels; there is never a suggestion that there is any conflict between the stern commands of Our Divine Lord and His tender Love for mankind: nor is there any hint that the sometimes stern authority of His Church will be contrary to that Church's tender love for the human race.

The love of Our Lord, shining from the Cross, demands obedience: the love of the Catholic Church, breathing in her creeds, demands obedience too. It has been left for this modern age to invent a weak, sentimental love which is afraid to demand obedience, and therefore breaks up Society and the home.

OUR LORD'S PRAYER FOR HIS CHURCH.

But this is not all that Scripture tells us of the Church. In the seventeenth chapter of St. John, Our Blessed Lord reveals to us what was lying closest to His Heart concerning His Apostles and the Church of which they were to be the foundation. They are very precious words, for they are the last words spoken by Him in the presence of all His Apostles before His Death. Here we are deliberately given an insight into the Divine Mind, and into the depths of the Divine Purpose and Wisdom. What is the heart of the whole chapter? Unity: Unity both internal and external. It is a prayer for the Apostles and all their needs, culminating in a prayer that they may be one with a unity visible to all the world.

THE APOSTLES' BELIEF IN OUR LORD'S GODHEAD.

In the opening of the prayer Our Lord reveals that the supreme fact in His Mind with regard to His Apostles is that they are the men given unto Him by the Father, to whom He had shewn the full Revelation of that Father:

"I have manifested Thy Name unto the men which Thou gavest Me out of the world" (JOHN xvii, 6).

To them He has given the words which the Father had given Him; and as a result they had believed and known surely that He had come forth from His Father. That is to say they believed in His Divine Mission and Godhead:

"I have given unto them the words which Thou gavest Me; and they have received them, and have known surely that I came out from Thee, and they have believed that Thou didst send Me" (JOHN xvii, 8).

Having mentioned this central truth, namely His Godhead, and their belief in it, He then goes on to pray for something which could only spring from such a belief, He prays that His Apostles may be one with a unity as real as the Unity in the Godhead Itself:

"Holy Father, keep through Thine Own Name